A BIRTHDAY FOR GENERAL WASHINGTON

A BIRTHDAY FOR GENERAL WASHINGTON

A Play

By Johanna Johnston

Pictures by Marjorie Burgeson

A Golden Gate Junior Book
Childrens Press, Chicago

Johnnycake

Library of Congress Cataloging in Publication Data

Johnston, Johanna.
  A birthday for General Washington.

  "A Golden Gate junior book."
  SUMMARY: Dramatizes the events at George Washington's
Valley Forge headquarters on his birthday in 1778.
  1. Washington, George, Pres. U. S., 1732-1799 — Juvenile
drama. 2. Valley Forge, Pa. — Juvenile drama.
[1. Washington, George, Pres. U. S., 1732-1799 — Drama.
2. Valley Forge, Pa. — Drama. 3. United States — History —
Revolution, 1775-1783 — Drama.] I. Burgeson, Marjorie.
II. Title.
PN6120.H5J66   812'.5'4   75-38545
ISBN 0-516-08881-5

Characters

NARRATORS
Two Continental Soldiers

GEORGE WASHINGTON
Commander-in-Chief of the Continental Army

A LIEUTENANT
Attached to General Washington's Staff

MARTHA WASHINGTON

A CORPORAL
An aide to General Washington

MILLER GOODMAN

MISTRESS GOODMAN
The Miller's Wife

JONATHAN GOODMAN
A boy of eleven

ABIGAIL GOODMAN
A girl of nine

FOUR CONTINENTAL SOLDIERS

Lieutenant

Corporal

Two Continental
Soldiers

Martha
Washington

General
George Washington

Characters

Miller Goodman

Mistress Goodman

CORN MEAL

Soldiers

Jonathan

Abigail

PROLOGUE

The narrators, two Continental soldiers, enter and take their places in front of the curtain.

FIRST SOLDIER: It was the winter of 1778. We Americans had been fighting for our independence from England for almost three years.

SECOND SOLDIER: With George Washington as our commander-in-chief we had won some victories. But then came a time of defeat.

FIRST SOLDIER: The English captured New York City—then Philadelphia.

SECOND SOLDIER: Then cold weather came and General Washington led us to winter quarters on a lonely stretch of land called Valley Forge, some miles beyond Philadelphia.

FIRST SOLDIER: We cut down trees to build huts. We went about the countryside looking for food.

SECOND SOLDIER: But the supplies we were counting on getting from the Continental Congress and the different states did not come.

FIRST SOLDIER: We had no blankets against the cold. Our clothes were in rags, our shoes worn out. Worst of all, we did not have enough food.

SECOND SOLDIER: By the end of February we were calling it the starving time.

FIRST SOLDIER: Let us take you back to that time—to the farmhouse near the camp where General Washington had his headquarters.

ACT I
Headquarters of General George Washington
Valley Forge, 1778

❈ CURTAIN RISES ❈

WASHINGTON: Just a minute, Lieutenant. As soon as I seal this letter it will be ready.

LIEUTENANT: I will ride with it at once, sir. I should be in York here in Pennsylvania by tomorrow morning and will deliver it to Congress without delay.

WASHINGTON: Yes, I know you will use all speed. If only Congress would answer as quickly.

LIEUTENANT: Sir, sometimes I wonder. Is it possible that the Congress is losing faith in the cause of independence?

WASHINGTON: No, no, do not say so, Lieutenant! It has been a hard winter for the members of Congress also. They had to flee to York when the British took Philadelphia. Some of them have been ill.

LIEUTENANT: Still, they are quartered in warm houses. Their clothes are not in rags. They have shoes. They have *food*.

WASHINGTON: Yes, I know, Lieutenant.

LIEUTENANT: You write letter after letter, sir, telling them of our hardships here, but week after week goes by and we get no supplies.

(There is a knock on the door)

WASHINGTON: Come in.

(*Enter Martha Washington*)

MARTHA: Good afternoon, George. Good afternoon, Lieutenant.

WASHINGTON: Martha, do come in. The lieutenant is just leaving.

LIEUTENANT: Good afternoon, ma'am. I will be on my way, sir.

WASHINGTON: Very good.

(*Exit Lieutenant*)

WASHINGTON: What can I do for you, wife?

MARTHA: I would like it if you left that desk for half an hour and came to have a bite to eat with me.

WASHINGTON: I'm sorry, Martha. I still have many letters to write. I must write again to Governor Trumbull of Connecticut. He, at least, has always been helpful in the past.

MARTHA: George, I traveled here from Mount Vernon to see that you do not wear yourself out with work. You *must* rest now and then. Besides—have you forgotten? Today is your birthday.

WASHINGTON: My birthday! I think I would rather forget it, Martha. Half of the soldiers are walking barefoot in the snow. They will have nothing to eat tonight but corn meal bread—johnnycake—no meat at all. It does not seem a day to celebrate.

(A knock on the door)

WASHINGTON: Come in.

(Enter Corporal)

WASHINGTON: Yes, Corporal. What is it?

CORPORAL: Bad news, sir. The wagonload of corn meal we were expecting from Goodman, the miller over on the east branch, has not arrived as promised. The men will not even have johnnycake for supper tonight.

MARTHA: Not even johnnycake!

CORPORAL: No, ma'am.

WASHINGTON: You see, Martha! It is not a day to celebrate. I cannot remember a day when things looked worse for our men and the American cause.

ACT II
Goodman's Mill, near Valley Forge

The two narrators enter and take their places before the curtain.

FIRST SOLDIER: A few miles away from the Valley Forge encampment is Goodman's mill. Outside, the mill wheel turns slowly in the half-frozen stream. A horse waits patiently between the shafts of a wagon.

SECOND SOLDIER: But inside the house the miller lies in pain. His wife, his son and his daughter are trying to comfort and ease him.

MISTRESS GOODMAN: Lie still, husband, so that the hot poultice on your back can do its work.

MILLER GOODMAN: But, wife, I *must* take the corn meal to the camp. The soldiers will go hungry if I don't.

MISTRESS GOODMAN: They have meal from other mills, I am sure. And after the way you wrenched your back loading the wagon you cannot go anywhere for days.

MILLER GOODMAN: No, no, they do not have enough meal at Valley Forge. The men are starving there. They do not have blankets or warm clothes—or shoes either. But at least I can take them some meal. I *must* go. (*He struggles to get up but winces and lies back.*) *Oooh!*

MISTRESS GOODMAN: Lie back—lie back.

JONATHAN: Father, I can take the wagon and deliver the meal.

MILLER: You, Jonathan? But you've never driven the wagon so far. You don't even know the way.

JONATHAN: I'll find the way. I can do it, Father. Anybody can tell me how to find General Washington.

ABIGAIL: And I'll go with him, to help.

MISTRESS GOODMAN: Oh, no!

JONATHAN: Please, Mother. I want to do something to help General Washington.

ABIGAIL: I do too. Oh, I can't bear to think that he is hungry and cold.

JONATHAN: Let us go, Father!

MILLER GOODMAN: You really think you can find the way?

JONATHAN: Oh yes—yes! Come, Abigail, let's get started.

ABIGAIL: Just one minute, Brother. There is something I have to take with me.

(Exit Abigail)

MISTRESS GOODMAN: Oh dear, oh dear! But at least you must bundle up well. Do you have your mittens?

(Enter Abigail. She wears a cape underneath which she is hiding something.)

ABIGAIL: All right, Jonathan, I'm ready.

JONATHAN: I'm ready too. Don't worry, Father. We'll get the corn meal to the General.

❧CURTAIN❧

ACT III
General Washington's Headquarters

Later that same afternoon.

MARTHA: Husband, I have never seen you so discouraged.

WASHINGTON: I do not know how much longer the men can endure their hardships, Martha.

MARTHA: You fear they will begin to desert.

WASHINGTON: Who could blame them? They have suffered for months! But what hurts me most is that our own countrymen do not care enough even to see that our soldiers have food to eat.

(There is a knock on the door.)

WASHINGTON: Come in.

(Enter Corporal)

CORPORAL: Sir, good news.

WASHINGTON: *(eagerly)*: Yes? What kind of news?

CORPORAL: The wagonload of corn meal arrived after all, sir. The men will eat tonight.

MARTHA: Oh, I am so glad!

WASHINGTON: Thank heaven! Not all our countrymen have forgotten us.

CORPORAL: Perhaps, sir, you might like to meet the wagon driver and his assistant?

WASHINGTON: Why, yes, certainly. Bring them in.

(Corporal goes to the door, signals to Abigail and Jonathan who enter.)

CORPORAL: Abigail and Jonathan Goodman, sir and ma'am.

MARTHA: Why, they are just children!

WASHINGTON: You two alone brought the corn meal?

JONATHAN: Sir, our father hurt his back so badly he could not come. But he knew how great was your need.

ABIGAIL: And he told us that you were cold, too. So I brought you this. I knitted it myself.. (*Takes a long woolen scarf from under her cape.*)

WASHINGTON: How can I thank you? How can I thank you both? You cannot know what it means to me to learn that America still has patriots—and young ones, too —our hope for the future. All at once, I again have hope for the American cause.

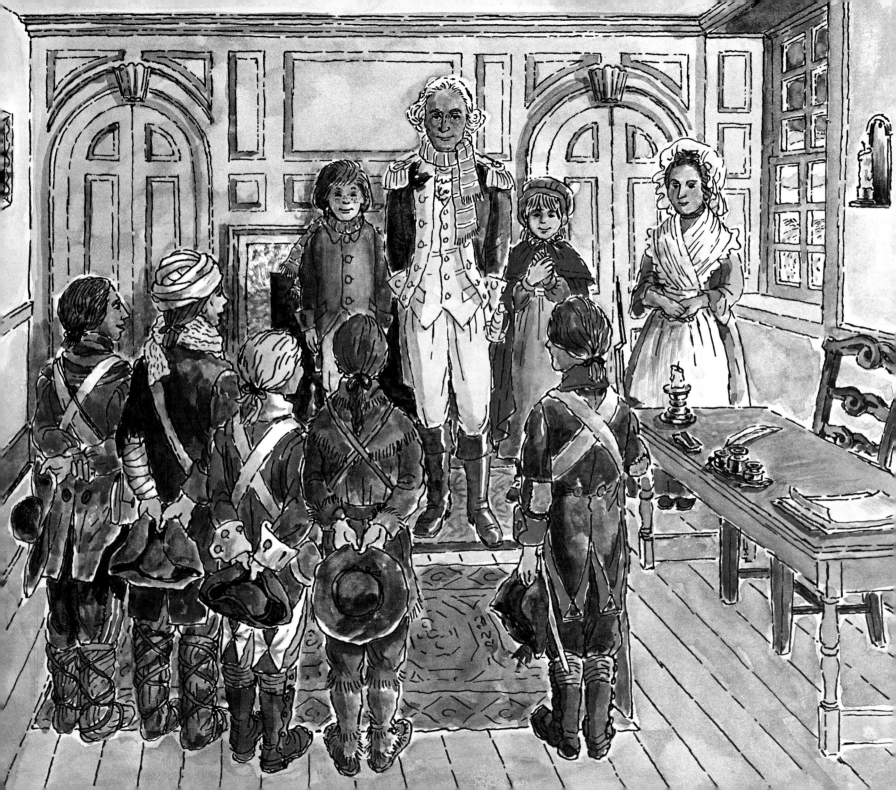

CORPORAL: Beg pardon, sir, but a group of soldiers are outside and wish to speak to you.

WASHINGTON: They have come to tell me they are hungry, I suppose. Well, at least we have some good news. Let them in.

(Corporal ushers in four ragged soldiers.)

FIRST SOLDIER: Sir, we have come with a special message from all the troops.

SECOND SOLDIER: We want you to know that we will stand by you and our cause until victory is won.

THIRD SOLDIER: Winter will not last forever. Better times will come.

FOURTH SOLDIER: We especially wanted to tell you so today, sir, because we have another message for you also. All together now!

ALL SOLDIERS: Happy birthday, General Washington! Happy birthday to you!

ABIGAIL: Oh, is it your birthday, sir?

JONATHAN: Really?

MARTHA: Yes, it is his birthday. And a little while ago he thought it was a sad day.

WASHINGTON: But now I'm beginning to think it is the happiest birthday of my life —thanks to all of you. Thanks to you, Jonathan and Abigail. Thanks to you, men, for giving me new hope and faith—the best birthday presents of all. Shall we celebrate with johnnycake?

CURTAIN

EPILOGUE

FIRST SOLDIER: Better times *did* come—very soon.

SECOND SOLDIER: Just a few days after the General's birthday word came that France had recognized the United States as a new and independent nation.

FIRST SOLDIER: Even better, the French were sending men and ships to help us fight the war.

SECOND SOLDIER: A famous soldier, Baron von Steuben, came from Germany to help train the American troops. Another fine soldier, Thaddeus Kosciosko, came from Poland.

FIRST SOLDIER: Supplies began to arrive at last.

SECOND SOLDIER: Spring came. The starving time was over. We were ready to fight again.

FIRST SOLDIER: The war did not end soon. But in many ways the General's birthday marked the turn to final victory.

SECOND SOLDIER: Washington would celebrate many more birthdays. Some as first President of the new nation, but none was quite so sad—then glad—as the one on February 22, 1778, at Valley Forge.

Feb. 22, 1778 ~ G. Washington

For General George Washington, Commander-in-Chief of the Continental Army, February 22, 1778, was not a happy day. The war for independence was not going well. Encamped for the winter at Valley Forge, Washington's men suffered badly from the cold. Their clothes were in rags, their shoes were worn out and, worst of all, they did not have enough to eat. No wonder the General had no heart to celebrate his birthday!

This is the background for a charming three-act play, written simply enough for young boys and girls to perform or to read for the enjoyment of a delightful story. How the day that began with so little promise turned out to be Washington's happiest birthday, thanks to the loyalty of his men and the courage of the two children who made a hazardous journey to bring him badly needed supplies, provides a heartwarming climax to a highly satisfying little drama. The lovely illustrations in full color add their own dimension.

JOHANNA JOHNSTON has long been interested in the beginnings of our country and has written a number of outstanding books for young readers about the many personalities who helped to shape its destiny. *Thomas Jefferson, His Many Talents* won her the distinguished Thomas Alva Edison Foundation award and was followed by *Together In America, A Special Bravery, Paul Cuffee, America's First Black Captain, The Challenge and The Answer*, and *The Indians and the Strangers* (Dodd, Mead). Miss Johnston writes for several age levels and is the author of *Who Found America?*, a book for very young readers, published by Childrens Press in 1973. A native of Chicago, she went to New York to write for radio and television and among her many scripts were plays for young children. She now devotes full time to writing books for both adult and juvenile audiences.

MARJORIE BURGESON is a distinguished painter and sculptor as well as a designer in the graphic arts field. Born in Seattle, she now lives in Claremont, California, with her husband and two young daughters. She spent her undergraduate days at Scripps College where she majored in art, then went on to Claremont Graduate School where she obtained the degree of Master of Fine Arts. She has won many prizes and her paintings and sculptures have been shown in a number of museums, including the San Francisco Museum of Art and the Los Angeles County Museum of Fine Arts. She is the illustrator of the play, *The Christmas Magic-Wagon*, published by Childrens Press in 1975.